PR

D0370632

Colemanballs
11

A selection of quotes,
most of which originally appeared
in PRIVATE EYE's
'Colemanballs' column.

Our thanks once again to all the readers
who sent us their contributions,
and to whom this book is dedicated.

COLEMANBALLS TOP TEN

PLACE	NAME	ENTRIES
1	DAVID COLEMAN	129
2	MURRAY WALKER	92
3	SIMON BATES	52
4	RON ATKINSON	47
5	KEVIN KEEGAN	46
6	TED LOWE	38
7	JOHN MOTSON	32
8	BRIAN MOORE	26
9	HARRY CARPENTER	22
10	BOBBY ROBSON	19

COMPOSITE TOTAL FIGURES COMPILED BY
THE NEASDEN INSTITUTE OF STATISTICS, E&OE

PRIVATE EYE

Colemanballs
11

Compiled and edited by
BARRY FANTONI

Illustrated by Larry

PRIVATE EYE

Published in Great Britain
by Private Eye Productions Ltd,
6 Carlisle Street, London W1D 3BN

©2002 Pressdram Ltd
ISBN 1 901784 30 4
Designed by Bridget Tisdall
Printed in Great Britain by
Cox and Wyman Ltd, Reading

Athletics

"Is that a grimace of pain in his right knee?"

DAVID COLEMAN

"She's not won a gold medal of any colour, has she?"

JAMES ANDREW

"And the hush of anticipation is rising to a crescendo..."

RON PICKERING

"She [Fiona May] only lost out on the gold medal because Niurka Montalvo, the Spanish athlete, jumped a longer distance than her."

DAVID COLEMAN

"When the American athletes were interviewed they were so sharp, so articulate – they were kind of wow..."

AINSLEY HARRIOTT

"That was an impressive run by the two English runners – one running for England and the other for Wales."

DAVID COLEMAN

"The girls are all very tired, they have had six big events between their legs already."

SALLY GUNNELL

"There you can see her parents. Her father died some time ago."

DAVID COLEMAN

"England couldn't have expected to win, but
they didn't expect to lose."

KAREN BROWN

"Moses Kiptanui – the 19-year-old Kenyan who
turned 20 a few weeks ago..."

DAVID COLEMAN

"I just want to get back to the shape I'm in now."

JAMIE BAULCH

"...just inching the bar up centimetre by centimetre"

BBC1

"She looks like the Olympic record-holder that she is."

DAVID COLEMAN

"...if she can keep her head and her legs together she shouldn't have too many problems."

BBC

"Jonathan Edwards – he has his faith, his health, his family, his children, but more importantly his Olympic medal."

BRIAN ALEXANDER

"Michael Johnson is the greatest athlete since sliced bread."

CYRIL REGIS

"I put that down to lack of inexperience."

DAVID COLEMAN

"You could be staring down the barrel of a gold medal."

ED HALL

"This is speed, power, grace – use whatever adjective you like about this woman."

STEVE CRAM

Boxing

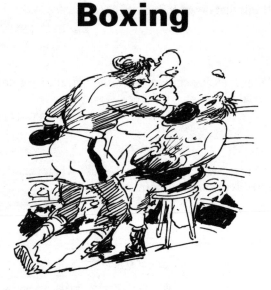

"I think Lewis will stop Tua somewhere between the ninth and tenth rounds."

AUDLEY HARRISON

"People talk about the altitude, but you've got to remember he's been on American time."

FRANK MALONEY

"We've dug our bed and we'll lie in it."

AUDLEY HARRISON

"People forget that Lennox Lewis is far from being whiter than white."

RADIO 5 LIVE

Cricket

"England have played pretty well... just their cricket let them down."

IAN SMITH

"Skipper Moin Khan has really earned his socks out there today."

CHRIS COWDREY

"...one of the Kiwi girls has been fingered by officials."

SPORTS PRESENTER, NEW ZEALAND

"Is cricket in danger of becoming a political football?"

KEVIN GREENING

"He's got two short legs breathing down his neck."

CHRISTOPHER MARTIN-JENKINS

"This ground is surprising – it holds about 60,000 but when there are around 30,000 in you get the feeling that it is half empty."

RAVI SHASTRI

"Bradman spent his latter years in Adelaide, sometimes watching his Australian contemporaries in action."

SKY NEWS

"Andy Caddick's shadow is longer than he is, and he's a very tall man."

JONATHAN AGNEW

"He [Courtney Walsh] has had a rest, Mikey, and a rest is as good as a break."

IAN BOTHAM

"Cricket corruption is a rolling stone – it's gathering moss all the time."

OLIVER HOLT

"Michael Vaughan has a long history in the game ahead of him."

MARK NICHOLAS

Football

"These things happen. Over a season, y'know, you'll get goals disallowed that are good, you'll get goals that are good disallowed. It happens."

KEVIN KEEGAN

"He's not the Carl Cort that we know he is."

BOBBY ROBSON

"He's the type of player the manager's either
going to keep or not keep next season."

ALVIN MARTIN

"The FA Cup is still domestically the best cup in the world."

GLENN HODDLE

"It's a tense time for managers. They have to exhume confidence."

GARY LINEKER

"Riding that tackle, he wiggled his hips like a daisy in the wind."

RADIO 5 LIVE

"He could have done a lot better there, but full marks to the lad."

RON ATKINSON

"[Ravanelli] was unlucky... or was it just bad luck?"

DES LYNAM

"He's got his legs back, of course, or his leg – he's always had one but now he's got two."

BOBBY ROBSON

"That was the way to nail the record to the mast..."

GLENN HODDLE

"You only get one opportunity of an England debut."

ALAN SHEARER

"There's going to be four or five teams battling for the top six spots."

CHRIS WADDLE

"... the midfield is outnumbered numerically."

RON ATKINSON

"It's getting tougher, teams are beating other teams left right and centre."

GLENN HODDLE

"We want a draw or as close as we can get to one."

BERWICK RANGERS FAN

"It's a tough month for Liverpool over the next five or six weeks."

ALAN GREEN

"Aston Villa are seventh in the League – that's almost as high as you can get without being one of the top six."

IAN PAYNE

"...and Tottenham ice their sublime cake with the ridiculous."

PETER DRURY

"I'm not going to drag it out or make a point, because points are pointless."

SIMON JORDAN

"Their away record is instantly forgettable. The 5-1 defeat and 7-nil defeat spring to mind."

RADIO 5 LIVE

"We have to be careful not to let our game not be the game we know it should be."

PAUL INCE

"There's a few tired limbs in the blue legs."

RON ATKINSON

"The midfield picks itself: Beckham, Scholes, Gerrard and A.N. Other."

PHIL NEAL

"This is the best Man United have played in Europe this season and, conversely, the opposition has been excellent."

RON ATKINSON

"Phil Thomson is Liverpool through and through. He's got red blood running through his veins."

RADIO 5 LIVE

"Anelka was travelling so fast that he couldn't keep his own feet."

CLIVE TYLDSLEY

"I have to sit down with him and see where we stand."

ARSENE WENGER

"Scotland don't have to score tonight, but they do have to win."

BILLY McNEILL

"…and Captain Beckham played like the Titanic…"

RADIO KENT

MANAGER'S ONION BAGS DO NOT REMOVE

"These managers all know their onions and cut their cloth accordingly."

MARK LAWRENSON

"England won 5-0 with Arsenal's Francis Jeffers scoring the winning goal."

CHANNEL 5 NEWS

"Gomes had scored four goals for Portugal against Andorra, including a hat-trick."

BILL O'HERLIHY

"Michael Owen isn't the tallest of lads, but his height more than makes up for that."

MARK LAWRENSON

"Even if he had scored for Alaves, it would have made no difference to the scoreline."

JERRY ARMSTRONG

"It's like the Sea of Galilee – the two defenders just parted."

MARK LAWRENSON

"Chelsea last won away on April Fools' Day – now it's Boxing Day, another great religious holiday."

DOMINIC JOHNSON

"They're in pole position, ie 3rd position, for the Champions' League."

MARK LAWRENSON

"The ball plunges up between the two of them as they meet."

RADIO 5 LIVE

"He's got a great future ahead. He's missed so much of it."

TERRY VENABLES

"This is a real cat and carrot situation."

DAVID PLEAT

"To be a great game, one of the teams has to score first."

MARK LAWRENSON

"There's Ottmar Hitzfeld, the two-year-old Bayern Munich Manager."

MIKE HILL

"To be honest, I can't remember him scoring a goal that wasn't memorable."

JEROME ANDERSON

"Andy Cole has at last broken his goal glut with his first goal for England."

CHANNEL 5

"All of a sudden they still keep playing that flat back four."

JOHN BERESFORD

"For me their biggest threat is when they get into the attacking part of the field."

RON ATKINSON

"They've conceded a lot of goals but their other problem is they've let a lot in."

GARY LINEKER

"Bobby Robson and Sven Goran Eriksson had a meeting before this match. Kieron Dyer will have been the name on two of their lips."

METRO RADIO

"[Dwight Yorke's] white boots were on fire against Arsenal and he'll be looking for them to reproduce tonight."

RON ATKINSON

"Two-nil was a dangerous lead to have..."

PETER BEARDSLEY

"...and it [the ball] just crept either side of the post."

CHRIS KAMARA

"[Bayern Munich] lost in the semi-finals of the Champions League to Real Madrid last year and the year before that were beaten in the final by Manchester United, so their European pedigree is second to none."

SIMON BROTHERTON

"And Scott Gemill has put Everton ahead in the big match between the bottom five."

STEVE RYDER

"...don't forget this club nearly went out of extinction last year."

ALLAN SMITH

"There's always one [FA Cup 3rd round upset] and the egg at the moment is heading squarely for Charlton's door!"

STEVE WILSON

"There's Thierry Henry, exploding like the French train that he is."

DAVID PLEAT

"My parents have been there for me, ever since I was about 7..."

DAVID BECKHAM

"Paulo di Canio is capable of scoring the goal he scored."

BRYAN ROBSON

"If it was a boxing match, you wouldn't know who was winning the game."

ITV

"Well, Clive, it's all about the two Ms, movement and positioning."

RON ATKINSON

"But he was a player that hasn't had to use his legs even when he was nineteen years of age because his first two yards were in his head."

GLENN HODDLE

"Ziege hits it high for Heskey who isn't playing."

ALAN GREEN

"If you're the chairman of a football club, and cocaine abuse is going on, you have to take a line on it."

GRAHAM SPIERS

"The defender was lightning slow."

RON ATKINSON

"England could have been 1-0 down on two occasions now."

JOHN MOTSON

"He [Anderlecht striker] hits it into the corner of the net as straight as a nut!"

DAVID PLEAT

"Without the ball, he [Totti] is a different player."

PETER BRACKLEY

"For some it's the ultimate job, for the others it's the last job."

KEVIN KEEGAN

"...so now Marian has the ball – let's see if she can open her legs to the Belles and show us all what she's made of..."

WOMEN'S CUP FINAL, BBC1

"He hasn't been the normal Paul Scholes today, and he's not the only one."

ALVIN MARTIN

"She was a born footballer, even when she was young."

EUROSPORT

"Quinn, for the umpteenth time, got his first goal of the current campaign."

BRIAN MOORE

"In some ways, cramp is worse than having a broken leg. But leukaemia is worse still. Probably."

KEVIN KEEGAN

"One accusation you can't throw at me is that I've always done my best."

ALAN SHEARER

"The tide is very much in our court now."

KEVIN KEEGAN

"Sometimes in football you have to score goals."
THIERRY HENRY

"There's a little triangle – five left-footed players."

RON ATKINSON

"The Germans only have one player under twenty-two and he's twenty-three."

KEVIN KEEGAN

"There's a slight doubt about only one player, and that's Tony Adams, who definitely won't be playing tomorrow."

KEVIN KEEGAN

"...and Shay Given has shaken off a broken nose to play."

BBC GRANDSTAND

"So you've nailed your mast to Gazza..."

RADIO 5 LIVE

"He [Steven Gerrard] looks as though he's been playing for England all his international career."

TREVOR BROOKING

"David O'Leary's poker face betrays the emotions..."

CLIVE TYLDESLEY

"It's got nothing to do with his ability. In fact, it has got to do with his ability."

BARRY VENISON

"...and the silence grew deeper and even louder..."

EUROSPORT

"...the Derby fans walking home absolutely silent in their cars."

ALAN BRAZIL

"They've maintained their unbeaten record between the legs."

BARRY DAVIES

"If you make the right decision, it's normally going to be the correct one."

DAVE BEASANT

"We have spent three matches chasing a football."

KEVIN KEEGAN

"People will look at Bowyer and Woodgate and say 'Well, there's no mud without flames'."

GORDON TAYLOR

"He's scored!! There's no end to the stoppage of this drama!"

ALAN PARRY

"It seems that they're playing with one leg tied together."

KENNY SANSOM

"I know that Gareth Barry has been told by Howard Wilkinson to take a long hard look at these with his left foot."

JOHN MOTSON

"It was one of those shots that just flew right along the floor..."

JIMMY ARMFIELD

"Every green seat has a bottom on it, and they've made some noise in here tonight."

JOHN RAWLING

"The first half was end-to-end stuff. In contrast, in this second half it's been one end to the other."

LOU MACARI

"We managed to wrong a few rights."

KEVIN KEEGAN

"And he (Zidane)... will have a private pool,
with a gardener thrown in."

DES CAHILL

"In the bottom nine positions of the league (D1) there are nine teams."

BBC1

"Cometh the hour, cometh the moment..."

RAY STUBBS

"We have run a marathon and fallen just short so we need to boost the squad to get us over that final hurdle."

JOHN RUDGE

"I want more from David Beckham. I want him to improve on perfection."

KEVIN KEEGAN

"Kevin Keegan said if he had a blank sheet of paper, five names would be on it..."

ALVIN MARTIN

"I have a definite sense of spirituality. I definitely want Brooklyn to be christened, but I don't know into what religion yet."

DAVID BECKHAM

"It's been mine and Roy Evans's job to really hold the baby and keep the ship afloat until the new board comes on board and we can get a course to which to steer to..."

PETER ROE

"A smoked salmon sandwich of a football match if ever there has been one."

PETER DRURY

"Hopefully, next season we will achieve a situation where we are playing with level goalposts."

CHRIS ROBERTSON

"Arsenal could have got away with a nil-nil if it wasn't for the two goals."

DES LYNAM

WorldCupballs

"Two questions – why were England so poor? And if they were poor – why?"

IAN PAYNE

"Apart from picking the ball out of the net, he hasn't had to make a save."

RON ATKINSON

"The Belgians will play like their fellow Scandinavians: Denmark and Sweden."

ANDY TOWNSEND

"Scholes is very influential for England at international level."

RON ATKINSON

"He's not George Best... but, then again, no one is."

CLIVE TYLDESLEY

"At international level, giving the ball away doesn't work too often."

RON ATKINSON

"...the number of chances they had before the goal they missed..."

MARK LAWRENSON

LINEKER: Do you think he [Rio Ferdinand] is a
natural defender?
O'LEARY: He could grow into one.

BBC1

"Some time in the 90 minutes they are going to
have to win the game."

TREVOR BROOKING

"The underdogs will start favourites for this match."

CRAIG BROWN

"It was a game of two halves, literally."

CHRIS POWELL

"You know when I say that things happen in matches? Well, it just happened there..."

RON ATKINSON

"Such a positive move by Uruguay – bringing 2 players off and putting 2 players on."

JOHN HELM

"That was in the past; we're in the future now."

DAVID BECKHAM

Golf

"The amputees' championship is coming off soon..."

PETER ALLIS

"Nick Faldo has created a Roman love pavilion for his forthcoming nuptials. He has incorporated a recessed ledge so that the happy couple can mount upon it during the ceremony."

RADIO 2

Horses

"She sadly passed away today, though three of her horses won today to cheer her up."

RADIO 5 LIVE

"In the last race favourite-backers would certainly have had their hearts in their chests."

DEREK THOMPSON

"He's drawn right in the middle – in other words, he is drawn right in the middle."

WILLIE CARSON

"I've had an interest in racing all my life – or longer really."

KEVIN KEEGAN

Ice Hockey

"I think we have enough talent to win if we don't rely on talent."

ICE HOCKEY COACH, POST BULLETIN, USA

In Memoriam
HRH The Queen
Mother

"We are witnessing the passing of the last eminent Victorian... something we won't see again for many decades."

JAMES FORLONG

"She was the most wonderful thing for jumping."

EX-JOCKEY LORD OAKSEY

"There will now be a minute's silence for Queen Elizabeth the First – the Queen Mother…"

PA SYSTEM, SOUTHEND UTD FC

"People are here, chatting and laughing – it's clearly a solemn occasion."

NICHOLAS WITCHELL

"I feel she will be remembered for her role during wartime. She stood alone against the mighty Nazi armies."

DAVID WINNICK MP

Literally

"I was literally nailed to my chair."

RADIO 4

"And a goal at this stage could, quite literally, be worth its weight in gold."

BBC WORLD SERVICE

"Andy Warhol's silk-screen paintings are literally the tip of the iceberg."

RADIO 4

"The police were literally swimming in a sea of red herrings..."

BBC1

"As the seconds tick down, Belgium are literally playing in time that doesn't exist."

ITV

"Andy Flower is literally carrying the whole of the Zimbabwe team with the bat."

DAVE HOUGHTON

Motor Sport

"We thought it was a foregone conclusion, and then it wasn't a foregone conclusion, but then it was a foregone conclusion again, and what a foregone conclusion it was."

CHANNEL 5

"Michael Schumacher – the finest driver ever to sit behind a Formula One car..."

BBC WORLD NEWS

"This circuit has everything. It's got gradients – both uphill and downhill."

MURRAY WALKER

"Michael Schumacher there, trying to go faster than himself..."

MARTIN BRUNDLE

"That's twice that has happened in the recent future..."

MURRAY WALKER

Music

"It wasn't on the initial CD, it was on the one before that..."

JONATHAN ROSS

"Cello players, like any great athlete, must keep their fingers working."

JULIAN LLOYD WEBBER

"And now the only band named after a
motorway – A1."

JOSIE D'ARBY

"I used to dream of being a pop star, but I never
dreamed I'd be one."

NEIL MORRISSEY

"Well, we wrote this song – but it didn't have
any words or a melody."

ROBBIE WILLIAMS

"At the age of only 19, Frederick Chopin gave his first live concert."

CLASSIC FM

Oddballs

"Religion used to be the opium of the people. Now we're looking to drugs as being the opium."

BISHOP JIM THOMPSON

"If people want to get out into the countryside or travel to London, they can go to Liverpool or Manchester for as little as £10."

RICHARD BRANSON

"This is something we just can't ever forget; and to be here helps me to remember."

VISITOR TO WTC, NEW YORK, BBC

"The Sydney Olympics transport plan relies heavily on the rail network. It is expected that 80% of every single spectator will arrive by train."

HUGH RIMINGTON

"You're probably the only news organisation in the world with reporters in Kabul. For news reporters, that's a position to die for."

ANDY COLLIER

"I'm a bit of a stickler for comprehendability."

BBC RADIO SCOTLAND

"...a shop that was founded in 1823 and still looks as old as ever..."

STEPHANIE HUGHES

"There's a lot of anti-Semitism, and it's not just against the Jewish."

CATE BLANCHETT

"Cars with fewer than one occupant will not be allowed into New York."

JOHN BURMAN

"You had to go inside the tent to understand where the tent was coming from."

TRACEY EMIN

"You believe that between then and now, in fact more recently than that…"

JEREMY PAXMAN

"It's too early to think about these things, but we can talk about them."

ROBERT ELMS

"The Pope has spoken of his unspeakable
horror."

RADIO 5 LIVE

"I got on with the Asian Community like a
house on fire."

FORMER LORD MAYOR OF BRADFORD

"...would it be hundreds of years, would it be centuries? Who knows..."

ANDY PEEBLES

"At the age of nine she [ballerina Alina Cojocaru] was born to dance."

NICHOLAS GLASS

"[Heather Mills] had her career cut short when she lost part of a leg..."

ROSIE MILLARD

"Is this an isolated incident, or is it just a one-off?"

JOHN SHIRES

"And for those of you who haven't seen the statue [of the naked Madonna], I have a photograph here in front of me."

SUE McGREGOR

"It's hard to know where to draw the line."

MARTIN CREED, TURNER PRIZE WINNER

"A lot of actresses have complained that as they get older the parts dry up."

JIMMY YOUNG

"...it seems the welfare of animals has been put on the back-burner."

WELSH RSPCA OFFICE

"You're on the horns of a two-edged blade!"

WALLY WEBB

"In this age of mobile phones, faxes and e-mails, we just don't communicate anymore..."

SUZY QUATRO

"And so he walks away with £250,000. That's the way to win a million on this show."

CHRIS TARRANT

"Six-and-a-half million people have visited the Dome and six-and-a-half left happy or happier."

P-Y GERBEAU

"Vauxhall's workers accused the chairman of being a Judas who washed his hands of them."

LONDON LIVE

"She [J.K. Rowling] has sold forty million copies in as many countries."

SUE LAWLEY

"The rainfall has been up to six inches that I've heard of, which is unheard of."

ARCHIE ROBERTSON

"Donald Bradman is not a tall man, and we know the Queen Mother is neither."

MARK NICHOLAS

"My former wife is now living with a woman of the same sex."

RADIO 4

"This is the final act in the never-ending drama."
EMMA HERD

"...many people felt that the paparazzi behaved like leeches, or – worse – bloodsuckers."
JOHN WILSON

"A lot of people have said that fibre is good... but if you look carefully at all the studies, the evidence is not so solid."
DR ROBERT GOODLAD

"Right now we have 13,000 prisoners sharing a cell designed for one person."

DAVID ROGAN

"Sniffer dogs are scouring Victoria station with a fine tooth comb."

ANTHONY BURLEIGH

"...and day will fade to dusk, lit by the smell of barbecues."

ELEANOR OLDROYD

"There were 150 drug-related deaths in Glasgow last year, an all-time high."

EMMA SIMPSON

"Sex with a mistress greatly increases the chances of having a stroke."

CHANNEL 5

"When the Deutschmark was at its peak the Germans went out and sold more Mercedes-Benz than any other car maker in the world."

LORD HANSON

"Can you confirm the suicide bomber was amongst the dead?"

NEWS 24

"This is a personal victory, and it's a personal victory for us all."

PETER HILLS

Politics

"Most motorists use roads rather than the Underground or railways..."

STEPHEN BYERS

"We have slammed shut the revolving door we found open."

BERTIE AHERN

"One thing we know for certain is that if he [Osama bin Laden] is not in Afghanistan, he is in another country or he is dead."

DONALD RUMSFELD

"...the longer this [indecision] goes on, the more the fig leaf of the economic tests is beginning to be exposed as rather hollow."

CHARLES KENNEDY

"Well, you can only fire at an open goal when you discover that it is a hand grenade you are kicking rather than the ball."

DAVID BLUNKETT

"At the end of the day in the morning there's not much else a teacher can do if the child doesn't turn up for school."

ESTELLE MORRIS

"A vote for the Lib Dems is a wasted vote –
only two parties can win this election."

WILLIAM HAGUE

"Iain Duncan Smith will stand shoulder to
shoulder behind Tony Blair at the present time."

CHANNEL 4 NEWS

"What we're doing is that which is currently do-able in the way that we're doing it."

DONALD RUMSFELD

"In a sense, Deng Xiaoping's death was inevitable, wasn't it?"

JON SNOW

"Israel is demanding that the Palestinian authorities arrest those people who have undertaken suicide bombings."

MIDDLE-EAST CORRESPONDENT

"In Scotland, the mass slaughter of farm animals has already begun. Further south, in Cumbria, a government minister has been dispatched."

CHANNEL 4 NEWS

"...John Prescott, flanked by his wife..."

KIRSTY WARK

"Now the press will be following Mandelson like a tonne of bricks."

DEREK DRAPER

"Saddam Hussein made a long, rambling broadcast, full of rhetorical questions, most of which remained unanswered."

RADIO 4

"[The Government should provide] fundamentals, like underwear for people at the bottom of society."

ROY HATTERSLEY

"Now's the time for those deaf ears to become unplugged; so they don't sleepwalk..."

TONY BANKS

"It is a cauldron in which the French are being roasted."

ANDREW MARR

Question
& Answer

SIMON MAYO: Ted Hughes, who was Poet
Laureate from 1984 until his death; Dead or
Alive?
CONTESTANT: Alive?

RADIO 1

PHONE-IN CALLER: 'The Pawnbroker', Rod –
is that the one about the small boy befriending a
stray dog?
ROD STEIGER: No. It's the one about a
pawnbroker.

RADIO 5 LIVE

WOMAN: My twin sister died when she was 54.
KILROY: How old were you then?

KILROY

RICHARD KEYES: Well, wasn't that the most
nail-biting and dramatic finale?
SHEARER: Yeah, especially at the end.

SKY SPORTS

SARA COX: So, do you notice anything different about me this morning?
NEWS ANCHOR: Ummmm... You're wearing the same t-shirt as yesterday?

RADIO 1

BOB WILSON: What about George Graham's record – seven trophies – that's second only to Sir Alex Ferguson.
ANDY TOWNSEND: That's right, Bob. George Graham's record is second to none.

ITV

INTERVIEWER: What do you think will happen if sperm donors' identities are revealed to their offspring?
FERTILITY EXPERT: It would be disastrous! They would just stop coming.

RADIO 4

JOHN CHAMPION: The question everyone is asking is why you didn't win by a greater margin.
ARSENE WENGER: It was because we didn't get a second goal.

BBC1

RICHARD FAULDS: I have so much to thank my parents for.
INTERVIEWER: Your mum and dad?
RICHARD FAULDS: Yes.

BBC1

TONY ADAMSON: Can you tell us how it feels to win or is it too early?
PADRAIG HARRINGTON: I can tell you exactly how it feels, I just can't find the words to describe it.

RADIO 5 LIVE

GERRY ANDERSON: These Thunderbirds models are expensive collectors' items. They cost £320 each.
INTERVIEWER: How much do they cost then?
GERRY ANDERSON: £320.

BBC1

JOHN LESLIE: What country is famous for tulips?
CONTESTANT: Holland.
JOHN LESLIE: Well, we'll give it to you... it's Amsterdam.

ITV

HENRY BLOFELD: Mrs Shepherd has made us some lovely Welsh cakes. What are they called, Don?
DON SHEPHERD: Welsh cakes, Henry.

RADIO 4

TERRY VENABLES: ...either it's a penalty or it's not.
DES LYNAM: And sometimes it's neither.

ITV

CALLER: It's Will Carling.
MOUNCE: What made you think it was him?
CALLER: His voice.

DOUGLAS MOUNCE

Rugby

"And there's Gregor Townsend's knee, looking very disappointed."

GAVIN HASTINGS

"We're reaping now what we failed to sow then."

CONOR FAUGHNAN

"And Matt Dawson, who has been dropped by England, is this morning in hospital suffering from concussion."

RADIO 4

"And Swansea have an uphill mountain to climb now."

JOHN HARDY

Skiing

"Alain Baxter faces an uphill struggle in the slalom tomorrow."

BBC1

Snooker

"At that pace he was always going to hit it or miss it."

JOHN VIRGO

"That's his strength – he invariably misses anything easy."

JOHN VIRGO

"Only he knows what he's thinking now. He'll be thinking that was his last chance to rescue the game."

JOHN VIRGO

"... I think you'll find that John Parrot was a victim of his own downfall there..."

STEVE DAVIS

"He couldn't have got any closer – although maybe he will this time."

JOHN VIRGO

Tennis

"I do sympathise with the problem of the net when you're hitting a volley. It's a real obstacle in the middle of the court."

VIRGINIA WADE

"Lleyton Hewitt... his two greatest strengths are his legs, his speed, his agility and his competitiveness..."

PAT CASH

"She just couldn't cope with the game that she didn't have."

VIRGINIA WADE

"He was a great tennis player, rather like a chess player, always trying to thread the ball through the eye of a needle."

TALK SPORT

"I had a feeling today that Venus Williams would either win or lose."

MARTINA NAVRATILOVA

"Tim Henman, I guess, is sitting in the locker room, pacing up and down."

JOHN INVERDALE

"Johnson looks more mentally tough than he appears."

RADIO 5 LIVE

"She [Dokic] left the court with a face as long as thunder."

JOHN INVERDALE

"Here we see Andre Sa, who, never having won a competitive match, has reached the Wimbledon quarter-final."

JOHN McENROE

"Andre Sa is playing close to his potential – maybe even above it."

BORIS BECKER

"It's been predictable, in the sense 'expect the unexpected'..."

JOHN McENROE

"He has great pressure on his shoulders internally."

RADIO 5 LIVE

"As Sampras prepares to put another notch in the history books..."

RICHARD EVANS